GW00771073

THE SECRET KEY
to The Emerald Tablets

Revealed by Thoth The Atlantean
With His Divine Feminine Counterpart

Rebecca Marina Messenger

The Secret Key to The Emerald Tablets
Revealed by Thoth The Atlantean With His Divine Feminine Counterpart

Copyright 2020 by Rebecca Marina Messenger
rebeccamarina.com

All rights reserved. No part of this publication may be reproduced, distributed, or transmitted in any form or by any means, including photocopying, recording, or other electronic or mechanical methods, without the prior written permission of the publisher, except in the case of brief quotations embodied in critical reviews and certain other noncommercial uses permitted by copyright law. For permission requests, email the publisher at Rebecca@rebeccamarina.com

ISBN: 978-0-9759390-8-6 (E-Book)
ISBN: 978-0-9759390-7-9 (Print)

Published by Celebration Healing Publishing

Book Interior and E-book Design by Amit Dey | amitdey2528@gmail.com

FREE GIFT

Audio "Connect with Your Heart's Desires"
visit rebeccamarina.com/resources

Other Books by Rebecca Marina Messenger:

1. Study Edition: The Emerald Tablets of Thoth The Atlantean - Available from Amazon, Barnes and Noble, and other Fine Bookstores

2. The Pleiadian Protocol for Reducing Excess Body Mass in Humans: The Never Before Revealed Secret Science from the Stars - Available on Amazon.com

3. Spiritually Decalcify the Pineal Gland - Available on Amazon.com

4. Cure White Sugar and Chocolate Cravings in One Hour: The Simple Secret You Need for Effortless Automatic Control Over Your Cravings - Available on Amazon.com

5. Book of Comfort 1: How the Earth Began, The Origin of Miracles, and a New Connection with Holy Spirit (Book of Comfort, The Messenger Series) Available on Amazon.com

THE SECRET KEY
to The Emerald Tablets

Revealed by Thoth The Atlantean
With His Divine Feminine Counterpart

This book is based on, and refers often to,
a most comprehensive book on the Complete
Emerald Tablets:

Study Edition: The Emerald Tablets of
Thoth The Atlantean

Prayer of Thoth

May your hearts be touched as you see the Truth of
who you are. Brothers and Sisters of the Light,
I welcome you to partake of this Wisdom. Read and
be still within your being. All is well with you.

Thoth - The Atlantean

Prayer of Seshat

Know that you are loved, welcomed, and embraced. The words in this text will bring you comfort in times of need, and in times of joy. Be still and KNOW... you have all you need already written on the walls of your heart.

Seshat - Divine Counterpart of Thoth,
Fairy Godmother of Egypt, Lady of Light

With Gratitude to Lee Wolf

Lee is much more than an Editor.

Her heart is in her work, and she CARES deeply about the content!

Lee has a keen interest in helping YOU, the reader, to get the most benefit from this writing.

Lee, I am forever grateful.

Dedicated to the Divine Feminine Principle

May Her Grace be revealed, and Her Love save us.

Let there be balance, at last, between the Divine Female Principle and the Divine Male Principle.

How to Use This Book

Say a prayer for guidance to the God of your understanding. Then, open to ANY page and be uplifted. Feel free to make notes in the margins... or in the many spaces provided. Ask questions - as this will open the door to your deeper understanding!

Introduction

This commentary and guidebook is eye-opening... because it brings in the guidance of the Divine Feminine, represented by Seshat, Wife/Consort of Thoth in Egypt and even to these modern times.

This is a more balanced union of Divine Masculine - united with the Divine Feminine - **which is the NEW Construct of Evolution!** Seshat was known as the "Fairy Godmother of Egypt" ... We could surely use a Fairy Godmother in these times!

Seshat tells me that she was also with Thoth in Atlantean times. Her name was Elnor in that period, and she was the Leader of the Atlantean Women Warriors of Light!

The Secret Key to The Emerald Tablets Is based on Emerald Tablet Three:
The Key Of Wisdom

Out of all of Thoth's Original Fifteen Emerald Tablets, why did Thoth request that Emerald Tablet Three be updated into modern English FIRST before any other?

Thoth said to me… "If one would understand the complete Emerald Tablets, let him return again and again to Emerald Tablet Three - The Key of Wisdom. In this Tablet, there is valuable advice that will serve to guide one through life. It could be called… 'The Key of Everything!'"

Thoth continues…

"There is a need for this Wisdom to be presented in BOTH the original text and plain English. My wife, Seshat, contributes Her Wisdom, and makes this the most completely understandable version possible. Both Seshat and I, present further guidance through newly Channeled material."

Table of Contents

List of Meditations

- Simple Meditation to Call Forth Your Inner Wisdom (See Chapter One)
- Meditation to Communicate with Your Heart (See Chapter Seven)

List of Exercises

- How to Increase the Gift of Discernment (See Chapter Three)
- Strengthen Your "Gut Instinct" (See Chapter Three)
- Exercise to Explore Your Heart's Desires (See Chapter Seven

Chapter One

Thoth Gives His Wisdom

From Emerald Tablet 3, Verse 1.

In the original translation from the Atlantean language, Thoth said...

I, Thoth, the Atlantean,
give of my Wisdom, give of my Knowledge,
give of my Power.
Freely I give to the children of men.
Give that they, too, might have Wisdom
to shine through the world
from the veil of the night.
Wisdom is Power and Power is Wisdom,
one with each other, perfecting the whole.

Thoth's Commentary, In Modern English:

Wisdom and Power MUST go together, for Power without Wisdom, is a destructive force. I am ready to teach anyone who will be still and listen. All that is needed is already there... on the walls of your heart. It is in the stillness, that Knowledge is revealed.

It is when one realizes that one is already Divine, that true Power begins to emerge. It takes courage to claim this inner power. It takes courage to claim your Divinity! It takes courage to buck the system that is currently in place - the practice of always looking outside of yourself for the answers. It is my prayer that you will tune into your own vast store-house of Knowledge... and allow that Wisdom to come forth.

You see, we are already connected. You are intimately connected to every Light Being that comes to your awareness! There is no need for feeling "less-than"... there is only a need for taking time each day to be quiet, and to allow that Wisdom to burst forth.

Seshat Contributes Her Wisdom:

It gives me great joy to be joining with Thoth in this transmission. Yes, it was He, Thoth, who wrote the Emerald Tablets over 36,000 years ago.

Yet, it was I, Seshat, who gave HIM the Strength and Support needed, to keep returning again and again to be your teacher.

In the days of Atlantis, I was known as Elnor, Leader of the Atlantean Warrior Women of Light. In the Egyptian lifetimes that Thoth and I shared together, I became known as Seshat. We partnered to do many wonderful things for the people of those times.

Question from Rebecca to Seshat: Why Didn't Thoth Write about You in the Original Tablets?

Answer: He did, in the Original Tablets, I am known as "The Lady of Light" (Tablet Ten, verses 21 to 27*). This account tells the story of how I was taken prisoner by the Dark Lords of Arulu.

It was Thoth who came to my defense and rescued me from the Dark Lords.

Such a daring feat demanded an extraordinarily powerful Sacred Ceremony! Thoth donned robes of purple and gold. He then beat a secret rhythm on a drum made of serpent skin.

Upon His head was a crown of silver, as He spoke the sacred words that the Dark Lords COULD NOT disobey!

Preparation for such a fearless rescue, required Thoth to pass time and time again through purification fires. He fasted from BOTH food and water for days, in order to gain sufficient spiritual power, to be able to prevail against the Dark Lords of Arulu.

These Evil Entities HAD to step aside and release me, so fierce was the Power and Authority of Thoth!

It is my honor to take part in this next step forward, in getting the timeless Wisdom of The Emerald Tablets out to the world.

In reading Emerald Tablet Three... you will experience an awakening within your DNA and cellular structure.

Even when the words do not make sense to your rational mind, your Spirit mind is dancing with glee!

It is recommended to focus time and again on Tablet Three: The Key of Wisdom... for it is most relevant to modern life.

Gaining knowledge of Tablet Three opens the doors of understanding to all of the writings of Thoth, The Atlantean.

Indeed, Tablet Three IS a KEY to All!

*Rebecca Marina Messenger makes reference to her first book - which contains the original text of all Fifteen of The Emerald Tablets -
Study Edition: The Emerald Tablets of Thoth The Atlantean - This is available from Amazon, Barnes and Noble, and other Fine Bookstores.

Simple Meditation to Call Forth Your Inner Wisdom:

Take a deep breath in and slowly release it.

Relax.

Use your eyeballs to assist in going into the deeper Alpha brain-wave state.

As you relax... roll your eyes three times in a clockwise direction... next, roll your eyes three times in a counterclockwise direction.

Now... while keeping your head still, roll both eyeballs upward, as if trying to look at the ceiling.

Next, take three breaths in and out slowly.

Relax.

Put your awareness on your physical heart center. Know that it is beating faithfully for you.

Appreciate your heart and the blood that constantly flows throughout your body.

Be still and relax.

With your attention still on your physical heart… imagine that you can see ancient tablets filled with Wisdom that are etched on the walls of your heart.

No need to do anything, simply acknowledge that these tablets are YOURS! On the walls of your heart are the records of Wisdom that you chose to bring forth into this lifetime.

These tablets of Wisdom have been brought forward from every past lifetime. There is nothing needed outside of yourself.

As you tune into your heart, be aware that every Light Being that you can imagine, is already a part of this Wisdom.

Imagine that the Light Beings are SPEAKING to you now...

"We are the accelerators of Wisdom. Yes, we help you to increase your awareness... yet, we are not more powerful than you. We are a bit more evolved because of being aware of you, even before you were aware of us, in this lifetime.

We are indeed ONE, and ALL BEINGS of LIGHT are now at YOUR service."

Slowly come back to awareness…

Now you know that you have access to all of the Wisdom you need… ready to be called forth whenever you need it. You have every Light Being ready to serve WITH you whenever you call!

Remember, the key to true Wisdom is achieving a still, quiet mind... and listening to the voice of your heart.

Chapter Two

Wisdom Can Come From Unexpected Places

From Tablet 3, Verse 2.

In the original translation from the Atlantean language, Thoth said...

Be thou not proud, O man, in thy Wisdom.
Discourse with the ignorant as well as the wise.

If one comes to thee full of knowledge,
listen and heed, for Wisdom is all.

Thoth's Commentary, in Modern English:

There is no need to get into false pride, because you have discovered your Wisdom. You can learn from the ignorant, as well as the wise.

It is when one gets puffed up with self-importance, that you miss the gift of understanding.

Even the most foolish person has SOME nuggets of Wisdom! Then again… if a person who is wise comes to you - and your heart resonates with their Wisdom - be still and listen.

Their Wisdom will awaken further understanding in you! For there are many "Key Masters" on the Earth today.

Even the most foolish person may have a soul con- tract to be a part of YOUR further awakening.

Always listen with your heart. Recognize truth only with your heart. For ONLY the heart can be trusted.

Seshat Contributes Her Wisdom:

Well has spoken my Beloved Thoth, yet I would add another aspect...

Seek not to find Wisdom entirely from the lips of men... or those in authority. Ask - and pay heed - to the most humble of Maidens.

For in the heart of a woman, there is much tender- ness, much understanding... that is not brought about by false pride. Women have long sought to be recognized and heard.

Great good and much advancement can be achieved when equal value is given to the female, as is given to the male. United Wisdom of both male and female, leads to a balanced understanding. This contributes to the forward progress of humanity.

Chapter Three

Curses, Sunlight, and Increasing Your Discernment

From Tablet 3, Verse 3.

In the original translation from the Atlantean language, Thoth said...

Keep thou not silent when evil is spoken,
for Truth, like the sunlight, shines above all.

Thoth's Commentary, in Modern English:

Evil words are like curses spewing forth from the lips of the unwise.
When you hear evil words spoken, and feel that knotting in your "gut" … speak up in defense of the Light.

You KNOW how to recognize when one is speaking curse-like words of evil. As you quietly speak your truth… Light shall prevail. This is a chance for others listening to hear the Truth.

Truth resonates!
Lies and evil judgments bring a person's Spirit down…

Here is a simple measure of Truth -
Do the words spoken lift you up?
Or ... do the words spoken bring you down?

Seshat Contributes Her Wisdom:

You have a chance to right the wrongs, spoken by those who would spread lies or harsh judgments. YOU can be the one... to come to the defense of a victim of untruth.

When a gossipmonger is confronted by a Light-Warrior of Truth, they will quickly back down. For a gossipmonger only gains power when they are heard and agreed with.

Evil stirs up more evil, and yet, let us have mercy on the one spewing the gossip. It is only due to their lack of self-confidence, that they turn to sensational gossip to attract attention.

Many of those who speak evil could be plagued by chaos entities. These beings always seek to stir up MORE turmoil to feed upon.

You can speak your Truth without being drawn into a heated dispute, by using your God-given gift of Discernment.

From Rebecca - My Definition of Gossip:

There is a difference between gossiping about him/her or **discussing** a person's situation.

For example, a mother may discuss her child's behavior with a trusted friend, hoping to gain some insight as to how to better parent. This is certainly not gossip … It is a sincere inquiry.

Your heart will KNOW when you have pure intent, or when you are sneaking in a few "barbs."
It is sometimes human nature to get satisfaction from putting someone else down. This is likely due to our need to feel a bit superior! Forgive yourself for that and pay more attention to your heart.

Or - Follow the Advice of the Great Philosopher, Socrates:

1. Is what you want to say the absolute truth? Are you sure?
2. Is what you want to say good or kind?
3. Is what you want to say useful or necessary?

Socrates said: *"If what you want to say is neither true, good, kind, useful nor necessary... there is no need to say anything at all."*

Exercise: How to Increase Your Gift of Discernment, From Thoth and Seshat

Relax and drop to your Heart center.
Take three deep breaths in and out slowly.

Put your awareness on your Solar Plexus, for that is where Discernment will get your attention.

Repeat the Atlantean word Huertal three times. (Pronounced... Where - Tall)

Imagine clear Light cleansing and expanding your Solar Plexus chakra.
Now... remember a time when you had a STRONG "gut instinct" that something was NOT right.

It is our hope that you paid attention to this "gut warning", and acted accordingly. If you did not heed that warning… you already know that there may have been disastrous consequences.

Be aware of how that memory stirs feelings in your "gut" ... and then moves up to your heart.

Now, remember a time when you had a STRONG "gut instinct" that something was right!

Again, it is our hope that you heeded that instinct and acted accordingly.

This is how you develop better powers of Discernment!

Pay attention. Play with this exercise... remembering even more times that you had a "gut instinct", and either paid attention to it, or ignored it.

Written Exercise: Strengthen Your "Gut Instinct"

Go back to the previous exercise and write out the times that you had a "gut instinct" about something...

The time that I felt in my "gut" that I should NOT trust (fill in the blank)

_____

_____

_____

_____

What happened? Did you act on the instinct?

_____

_____

_____

_____

What do you wish you had done in that situation?

_____

_____

_____

_____

The time that I felt in my "gut" that I should DO (what)?

_____

_____

_____

What happened? Did you act on the instinct?

_____

_____

_____

What do you wish you had done in that situation?

_____

_____

_____

Examples from Personal Experiences: (All names changed to protect anonymity.)

A client, Mara, shared with me a story from her life that is a wonderful example of having a "gut instinct" about a situation… and NOT following the guidance.

Mara is a talented Healer and Lightworker. She is very intuitive, and has used her gifts to help many people and animals for many years. But in one situation… where she was receiving definite "vibes" that something was NOT right, she ignored them and felt that she must be wrong.

Mara refused to believe that a person could ever possibly do what this person was doing. She even told the person of her suspicions… but he reassured her that he would never do what she suspected.

Well... he did - indeed - do what she suspected - and worse!

This "confidence man" was skillful in gaining the trust of his intended "targets" ... and swindled her, along with other members of her family, out of a lot of money.

This happened a long time ago, but Mara learned the hard lesson of trusting your "gut instinct" and following clear guidance.

Another client relates this story:

Betty met a man online. He said all the right things that her heart had longed to hear. So, she agreed to meet him… even though she had what she described as a "funny feeling" in her "gut." She ignored that feeling!

As she drove to meet him, the "funny feeling" increased dramatically. Still, she ignored the feeling, thinking that no one could have said all those wonderful words to her... if they were not true.

When Betty arrived at the meeting place and looked into his eyes… it was as if she were looking into the eyes of pure evil!

Finally, Betty got the "loud and clear" message - "This man is evil and intends to do me harm!"

She quickly excused herself and left the meeting, feeling lucky to be alive! It was ONLY when she looked into the face of darkness... that she realized how clearly her "gut instinct" had been trying to warn her.

You see… "gut instinct" does not usually follow a logical path. A person can be admired by many others... they can say all the right things, sounding very sincere, and yet be completely untrustworthy!

Pay attention to your own "gut instinct." DO NOT listen to others, who tell you that you are wrong not to trust a certain person or situation.

Your intuition KNOWS what is RIGHT for YOU!

A note about psychopaths…

A psychopath can have the uncanny ability to tap into a target's **subconscious desires.**

When the target hears their very thoughts and desires spoken by the psychopath… they easily shut off their own intuition, assuming that it has to be wrong.

This is exactly how many psychopaths lure their intended targets into trusting them.

If you are dealing with a suspected psychopath, TRUST your "gut instinct," and NOT the honeyed words they speak!

Chapter Four

Law, Punishment and Freedom

From Tablet 3, Verse 4.

In the original translation from the Atlantean language, Thoth said...

He who over-steppeth the Law shall be punished, for only through Law comes the Freedom of men.

Thoth's Commentary, in Modern English:

The Natural Laws of the Universe are in place for the safety and evolution of mankind, animals, plants... the entire solar system.

Here are Twelve Laws that Always Apply:

1. **The Law of Divine Oneness -**
   We are all ONE and interconnected.

2. The Law of Vibration -

All particles of all substances are in constant movement.

3. The Law of Correspondence -

Patterns constantly repeat themselves throughout the Universe on both large and small scales.

4. The Law of Attraction -

Like always attracts like.

5. The Law of Inspired Action -

Actively pursue your goals when inspiration strikes you. True inspiration is always followed by a surge of energy.

6. The Law of Perpetual Transmutation of Energy -

Everything is constantly changing. Some changes are not noticed, as they are occurring at cellular or atomic levels. They ARE changing, nonetheless.

7. The Law of Cause and Effect -

All actions have a corresponding reaction.

8. The Law of Compensation -

You will receive back what you give out, in kind. You reap what you sow.

9. **The Law of Relativity -**

Nothing is either good or bad, until it is compared to something else. You may consider yourself poor, until you compare yourself to a homeless person.

10. **The Law of Polarity -**

Everything has an opposite. Scarcity helps you to appreciate abundance. Dark helps you to appreciate Light, etc.

11. **The Law of Rhythm -**

All things occur in cycles. Nothing is permanent.

12. **The Law of Gender -**

There are two major types of energy… Yin/Yang, Male/Female. You can activate the Law of Gender more fully by using your imagination.

To activate masculine energy, imagine things **going AWAY** from you.

To activate feminine energy, imagine things **coming TOWARD** you! Imagine BAD things going AWAY (masculine). Imagine GOOD things COMING (feminine).

Thoth Continues…

When you work in harmony with these laws, your life, and the life of the planet… **is always balanced!**

When you ignore these laws… you create your own dis-harmony/dis-ease.

There is no punishment outside of yourself.

Everything is the consequence of either keeping the Natural Laws or going against these Laws.

Seshat Contributes Her Wisdom:

Many people live in fear, that there is an angry God out there who is waiting to punish them.

There is no Deity of Light who would ever wish to bring harm upon any person, place, animal, plant, sea, or any being ever!

As you learn to embrace the Natural Laws… you more easily embrace your own Divinity. Let us dwell together in harmony.

Even the Divine Beings of Light must abide by the Natural Laws. These Laws are not meant to sub-jugate humans… but to lift them up, in the glory of abundant living!

Chapter Five

Cause No Fear

From Tablet 3, Verse 5.

In the original translation from the Atlantean language, Thoth said...

Cause thou not fear, for fear is a bondage,
a fetter that binds the darkness to men.

Thoth's Commentary, in Modern English:

DO NOT be the cause of striking fear into the hearts of man nor beast.

Fear causes loss of Liberty... and is the opposite of Freedom.

Fear keeps all in a space of darkness.
In darkness, one cannot thrive.

Seshat Contributes Her Wisdom:

There are those who seek to rule, by instilling fear in the hearts and minds of others.

This is NOT of the Light and will no longer be tolerated!

It is NOW time for the Warriors of Light to rise up and say... **NO MORE!**

Those who seek to control by fear tactics, are insecure in their own Power. Yes, we can have mercy on them, and pray for their highest outcomes.

However, it is up to each individual to proclaim their own sovereignty!

Each one of us carries the Light of Divinity within. That Light can no longer be overcome by the spirit of fear, or by those seeking to control.

Fear is the opposite of Love. Seek Love and Mercy, and long shall be the days of your Life. Happy shall your heart be. True wealth begins and ends, with the capacity to **Love.**

Chapter Six

Follow Your Heart

From Tablet 3, Verse 6.

In the original translation from the Atlantean language, Thoth said…

Follow thine heart during thy lifetime.
Do thou more than is commanded of thee.

Thoth's Commentary, in Modern English:

Follow after the true desires of your heart. All that you desire deeply in your heart, is that which you planned before this physical incarnation.

You will always be steered in the direction that your soul is longing for...as long as you follow your heart!

Do not try to get away with doing as little as possible. You will feel like a cowardly cheat if you live your life in this way.

When you go the extra mile, doing more than has even been asked of you, true sensations of joy in accomplishment will be yours.

This leads to a sense of satisfaction of self, that raises your vibrations like nothing else!

You will hear the words, "Well done thou good and faithful servant", singing in your heart. Not only will you be satisfied with yourself... you will KNOW that your Creator is satisfied as well.

Seshat Contributes Her Wisdom:

It is a great discovery, when you find that the very things that bring you joy... are the things that you planned to accomplish in this lifetime.

The path to fulfillment is in following the inner promptings of your heart.

Just as your intuition may give you warnings via your "gut" - so your heart gives you promptings through the energy of **joy.**

Follow your joy indeed! Resist feeling any guilt, for daydreaming about having the desires of your heart. That which you give your attention to... grows.

Nothing could serve your Spiritual growth better, than to daydream, even fantasize, about having the desires of your heart!

When a task is requested of you, do more than you are asked to do, as long as you do it with a cheerful heart and a smile on your face.

Going the extra mile and maintaining a cheerful heart... springboards you into a feeling of "satisfaction with self."

It is GOOD to be able to pat yourself on the back sometimes and KNOW that you did more than was required of you.

Chapter Seven

True Riches are Found in the Heart

From Tablet 3, Verse 7.

In the original translation from the Atlantean language, Thoth said...

When thou hast gained riches,
follow thou thine heart,
for all these are of no avail if thine heart be weary.

Diminish thou not the time of following thine heart.
It is abhorred of the soul.

Thoth's Commentary, in Modern English:

Even after you obtain riches, always return to following the path of your heart. Riches are of no value to anyone... if the heart is not honored. Never hesitate to turn again and again to your inner Wisdom. Your very soul will shrink away in horror if you go against the guidance of your heart.

Only the heart knows how to obtain true happiness. Be not fooled into thinking that pleasure can only be found in riches. Yes, money can improve the quality of your life, and wealth is good to accumulate.

Wealth without happiness, is like sitting down to a sumptuous banquet… and having a miserable toothache that prevents you from enjoying it - or even partaking.

Seshat Contributes Her Wisdom:

Precious Brothers and Sisters… Can you see the Wisdom in what my Beloved Thoth has put forth?

Allow yourself to feast upon the happiness that can only be found in your heart.

If you find yourself in a place of NOT having happiness... turn again to the stillness within your heart.

Do not try to move past the sadness into happiness, until you have sat awhile in communion with your heart.
Even sadness has something to teach you.

Meditation to Communicate with your Heart's Desires:

For FREE Audio of this Meditation, visit rebeccamarina.com/resources (Listening Recommended)
Before doing this meditation, think a bit about the desires that you have for your life.
Relax.

Place your awareness on your physical heart.
Let the worries about your life float away.
See the red blood pumping with ease throughout all of the chambers of your heart.

Relax.

Imagine that your heart has a little house right in the middle. It is a beautiful house! So tiny and comfortable...

Imagine that there are three rooms in the house that are just for your "heart's desires."

You can see the three rooms with the words "heart's desires" written on each door.

Go slowly over to door Number One. This is your most precious desire.
Open the door, what is on the other side?

How does it look?
How does it feel?
See yourself having it… how does that feel to you?

Now do the same with door Number Two.
Go over to that door, this is another heart's desire
that you have.
What is behind that door?

How does it look?
How does it feel?

See yourself having it… how does that feel to you?

You have one more door to explore.
Perhaps this is a secret desire that you are too afraid
to even admit.

Open that door slowly.
Let the joy surge as you proclaim the secret desire to
be yours!
How does it look?

How does it feel?
See yourself having it… how does that feel to you?

Now come back and write down what was behind the three doors.

_____

_____

_____

_____

_____

_____

_____

Know that if your heart desires it... then it is Divine Will for you to have it. Your desires are your roadmap to happiness, and the fulfillment of your soul purpose.

Written Exercise: Explore your Heart's Desires:

Have pen and paper ready.
Write down some of the heart's desires that you have had in your lifetime.

Desires:

_____

_____

_____

_____

_____

Our desires change with our timelines. That which our heart desired as a child, is usually NOT the same desire we would have as an adult.

Think of a time when you really pursued your desires and made them come true. How did that feel?

Write down the desires, as well as the feelings you had.

_____

_____

_____

_____

_____

Think of a time when you had a deep desire and it never came to fruition.

How did that feel?

Write down the desires, as well as the feelings you had.

_____

_____

_____

_____

_____

This exercise helps you to become aware of the importance of your heart's desires... and the ability those desires have to bring you happiness and satisfaction.

Chapter Eight

Love, Guidance and the Straight Path

From Tablet 3, Verse 8.

In the original translation from the Atlantean language, Thoth said...

They that are guided go not astray,
but they that are lost cannot find a straight path.

If thou go among men, make for thyself, Love,
the beginning and end of the heart.

Thoth's Commentary, in Modern English:

The heart and the "gut", are the guidance systems that we have been speaking about.

If you do not pay attention to either the heart or the "gut", you will surely feel lost!

As you go about your daily life, always let Love be the motive for all that you do.

Seshat Contributes Her Wisdom:

In every moment be asking yourself… Does this action feel loving or NOT loving? Am I doing this action from a place of Love and highest good for all, including myself?

Most importantly, ask yourself… Am I loving myself and my soul's course? You are only responsible for your own soul's journey.

As much as you might seek to influence or change the journey of another, the only true path for you, is your own personal path.

Find yourself at peace... in the journey of your own soul, knowing that you chose this exact time to come into this exact incarnation.

Chapter Nine

Listen and Judge Not

From Tablet 3, Verse 9.

In the original translation from the Atlantean language, Thoth said…

If one cometh unto thee for counsel,
let him speak freely,
that the thing
for which he hath come to thee may be done.

If he hesitates to open his heart to thee,
it is because thou, the judge, doeth the wrong.

Thoth's Commentary, in Modern English:

When someone comes to you for advice, put aside your own judgment… as you hear them out.

If you are in a place to dispense Wisdom, wait until the person has poured out their heart to you... before speaking your opinion.

If a person values your advice enough to honor you by requesting your input, honor THEM by keeping silent until you have weighed all in your heart.

Encourage them to tune into their own heart for guidance from within.
If the person hesitates… it is because they feel the JUDGMENT energy that is coming from you!

Seshat Contributes Her Wisdom:

It is a real gift, to keep silent as you allow another person to confide in you… especially when they come to you for advice.

Often, just the act of speaking the problem out loud... will cause the person to KNOW what course of action they should take.

If a person hesitates when genuinely seeking your counsel, it is due to the condemning energy that you may be giving off.

If you cannot look at an issue with an open mind, it is better to confess this to the person asking advice.

Simply say… I am not the best person from whom to seek advice on this topic, as I have my own triggers/ issues around this.

Admitting that you have your own set of judgments does not lower you… it makes you more human.

False pride is detrimental. Your honesty will help them, much more than faulty advice tainted by your own harsh judgments.

Chapter Ten

Gossip Hinders Wisdom

From Tablet 3, Verse 10.

In the original translation from the Atlantean language, Thoth said…

Repeat thou not extravagant speech,
neither listen thou to it,
for it is the utterance of one not in equilibrium.

Speak thou not of it,
so that he before thee may know Wisdom.

Thoth's Commentary, in Modern English:

Do not repeat gossip. Do not even listen to it.
For gossip is spoken by one who is not in balance.
Do not repeat the things said… but gently keep silent.

The one seeking to stir up unrest by vain words... will
realize that there is no value in idle gossip. This may
cause them to turn their own thoughts inward... and
become wiser.

Seshat Contributes Her Wisdom:

"Idle words" is a practice most commonly attributed to women.
Yet, both males and females often seek to gain attention, or a sense of importance, by spreading gossip.

As you react with an air of indifference… or appear completely disinterested, the one seeking to gossip will fall silent.

For your own progression forward, it is always good to ask:
Are these words uplifting?
Are these words kind?
How does my heart feel as I speak them?

It does not matter if the words are factual. It profits your soul nothing if words are uttered in spite.

Chapter Eleven

Silence is Golden

From Tablet 3, Verse 11.

In the original translation from the Atlantean language, Thoth said...

Silence is of great profit.
An abundance of speech profiteth nothing.

Thoth's Commentary, in Modern English:

Knowing when to keep silent, is a marker of greater Wisdom. Talking incessantly is of no value... and wears the patience thin!

Seshat Contributes Her Wisdom:

Only in Silence, can the true Wisdom of the heart be brought forward. When one is constantly speaking... there is no time for reflection.

As one learns to be calm and quiet, inner Wisdom has a clear path to surface. Constant input and output… with no time left for Silence, is detrimental to the soul.

Chapter Twelve

Pride Cometh Before a Fall

From Tablet 3, Verse 12.

In the original translation from the Atlantean language, Thoth said...

Exalt not thine heart above the children of men, lest it be brought lower than the dust.

Thoth's Commentary, in Modern English:

Do not think that you are greater, or more exalted, than any other man or woman. When you enter into a sense of false pride... you are an easy target for self-humiliation.

Know this, you are not greater than or less than, any other being. Perhaps you may be in a different place energetically.

Always return to the heart... and be in the space of mercy and tenderness for all.

Seshat Contributes Her Wisdom:

It can be easy to feel like you are better than your Brothers and Sisters… especially if you have spent a lot of time in Meditation and Prayer.

But this is simply your ego coming forth. It is times like these, when you realize just how far you still have to go in your evolution.

You can see how easy it is to get into a sense of false pride.

For this reason, please have mercy on those you see around you, who are struggling to evolve spiritually.

Hold the mirror up to your own face first... before judging others.

It is true that Light Workers can tend to get into a space of feeling superior. Perhaps, they feel more advanced because they dedicate an hour or two each day to meditation… while others do not. Each must be responsible for his/her own journey.

You cannot truly know what any Brother or Sister does, knows, or believes, within their own heart.

Chapter Thirteen

What Will You Be Known For?

From Tablet 3, Verse 13.

In the original translation from the Atlantean language, Thoth said…

If thou be great among men,
be honored for knowledge and gentleness.

Thoth's Commentary, in Modern English:

If you desire to be known as a great man or a great woman… let people see your gentleness. Yes, let people share freely in the knowledge that you have accumulated.

Lording knowledge over people, will never prove that you are a great person.
Perhaps people will fear you… yet, they will not come to you for counsel!

Always go back to your own heart and look for guidance as to *your* own purpose.

Why are <u>you</u> here?

Are you here to be known as someone great?
Or to be known as one who truly reached others,
through the Wisdom and gentleness of your heart?

Seshat Contributes Her Wisdom:

It takes a great heart to realize the importance of showing your Wisdom... along with gentleness.

To have a gentle heart does NOT equate with having a weak heart, or being a pushover!

Gentleness means... to handle people, life, animals, the earth, and all that you encounter, with a gentle approach.
Set this as your intention, and all will be well.

Those who truly KNOW, will see that a person willing to seek the gentle way... is far more powerful than one who would go about as a roaring lion!

It takes MORE power to see life through the non-threatening eyes of a gentle heart, than to always be poised to force your will upon others.

True Power is found within yourself. It includes your confidence in your own abilities, your own Divinity.

True Power never feels threatened!

Sit with this guidance. Pass it through the filter of your own heart.

Be still and KNOW.

Chapter Fourteen

Rely on Your Own Discernment

From Tablet 3, Verse 14.

In the original translation from the Atlantean language, Thoth said…

If thou seeketh to know the nature of a friend, ask not his companion, but pass a time alone with him.

Debate with him, testing his heart by his words and his bearing.

Thoth's Commentary, in Modern English:

Spending time with the person whom you wish to know more about, is the only fruitful way to gain understanding of that person.

Speak about several topics together… enjoy conversation, and you will easily be able to read his nature. You can tell, not only by his/her words, but by the vibrational essence which they exude.

Seshat Contributes Her Wisdom:

When getting to know a person, be sure that you put in the effort to spend time with them. To simply ask a companion about that person… could give you a faulty opinion.

Why? Because every person has their own filters. You are the one wanting to know more about the person, right?

Then only YOU can assess whether this is someone you desire to have in your inner circle… or not.

Spend time with them, without the judgments of another person clouding your vision. Pay attention to how you FEEL when you are connecting with this person.

Pay attention to your "gut"… and to your heart!
The heart will NEVER lie to you.

Remember how we talked about Discernment?
Pay attention to any red flags that are coming up… and always come from a place of being merciful.

Perhaps this person is in your path so that you can be a trusted advisor to them. If it is a love interest, remember that you are not looking for a "fixer upper," but a person in vibrational harmony with you.

Red flags, when considering a love interest, are meant as a warning that MUST be heeded!

We could go into that in greater detail in another book... for now, PAY ATTENTION and protect yourself from getting into energy-draining romantic relationships.

Chapter Fifteen

The Difference Between Hoarding and Sharing From the Heart

From Tablet 3, Verse 15.

In the original translation from the Atlantean language, Thoth said…

That which goeth into the store-house
must come forth,
and the things that are thine
must be shared with a friend.

Thoth's Commentary, in Modern English:

What you put away for a rainy day will wither and mold, if not used when need arises. It is far better to share what you have with those in need, than to hoard it all for yourself.

Hoarding is an emotional state, that extends far beyond money or wealth. If you allow the energy of hoarding to overtake your life, you will find yourself in an unhappy state. You may begin to hoard time, relationships, even energy. Be wary of this sneaky darkness.

If you see your Brother in need, take that which you have put aside, and share it with him. Always follow your guidance on this.

There are some who are in need as part of their life lesson and must come to their own understanding.

If every person gave when and where guided, there would be no poverty in the world. The Universe is always listening to the voices of those in need.

There is a Divine plan of giving and receiving for all of Life.

Sharing from guilt does NOT bring joy!
Sharing when guided brings about great joy!
A state of joy causes you to attract even more abundance!

Seshat Contributes Her Wisdom:

My Beloved Thoth has spoken well! I would add a few more things to consider.

We are all sources of food for something!
We all both give and receive Life and nourishment.

Consider this…
A plant receives rain and nourishment from the Earth.
We receive the plant as we eat it.

Perhaps the plant is food for animals, and they are also
consumed. Humans are a source of food for thousands
of parasites, bacteria, and viruses in every moment!

Let us take this into the realm of Spirit.

When humans exude negative energy… they
become food for chaos energies to feast upon. This
can be a trap, as the chaos energies stir up more
strife, in order to keep their food source growing.

Beings of Light are very attracted to humans when
they are in a state of happiness and bliss. They
warm themselves by the fire of your good energy.
Happiness begets more happiness.

It is GOOD to share happiness with a friend! When
you are in a happy state, reach out to a friend who
could use some uplifting words or energy.

The storehouse need not be thought of as only a
place for money. The storehouse of your energy… is
far more valuable.

For, with the right energy and the right state of mind,
much wealth of ALL things accumulates naturally!

Chapter Sixteen

Pity the Fool Who Resists Knowledge

From Tablet 3, Verse 16.

In the original translation from the Atlantean language, Thoth said…

Knowledge is regarded by the fool as ignorance, and the things that are profitable are to him hurtful.
He liveth in death.
It is therefore his food.

Thoth's Commentary, in Modern English:

A fool thinks he/she knows the Truth, even when their own life is in dis-array! It is as if he/she is so blinded by their own ego, that they refuse to accept any other point of view.

The fool suspects that the things that could help… are harmful. He/she does not listen, and rarely seeks counsel of the heart.

He/she lives a lie.

That lie is their sustenance... and it eats them alive!

Seshat Contributes Her Wisdom:

I plead for you to enter a state of mercy, when approaching someone who has this foolish type of personality.

Very often, when one is so turned away from knowledge, it is from a sense of insecurity.

They become so ensconced in defending their point of view, that they bring harm to themselves… all through ignorance.

Many who have a stubborn resistance to Truth, were influenced by false teachings in childhood.

Those holding this personality type, often hang their beliefs on doctrine, and believe fiercely that they have been taught well.

When conversing with one who "bristles up" as you present a different point of view… be wary. It is NOT your job to convince anyone of anything that they do not wish to see. Again, let us go back to the teaching about having a "gentle heart."

Plant a little seed if your Discernment tells you to do so, yet engage NOT in arguing. Doing that will only drain your priceless life-force energy.

There are plenty of people who DESIRE to know more Truth.

YOUR prayer is this… Divine, please guide me ONLY to those **that I am meant to help**.

Remember this, you are like a key that opens a lock, but only to those who are READY for YOUR guidance.

Chapter Seventeen

Overflowing Hearts Need No Words

From Tablet 3, Verse 17.

The wise man lets his heart overflow
but keeps silent his mouth.

Thoth's Commentary, in Modern English:

When your heart is overflowing with Love… no
speaking is needed. Your heart always speaks
louder than words!

Seshat Contributes Her Wisdom:

This is a truly short admonition, yet the wise would
do well to heed this Truth. You can do much good by
sitting in Silence… while sending out the vibrations
of pure Love from your heart!

Try this the next time you desire to let someone
know that they are loved. Sit and think of them…

holding them in your heart. Imagine actual waves of Love going out to them.

This is especially useful if you have had a disagreement with someone... and desire to make peace.

Sometimes, you may not FEEL Love for a person, and yet you still desire peace. In that case... be still, send thoughts of peace, and ask the presence of DIVINE LOVE to surround them.

Chapter Eighteen

Be FREE From the Bonds of Darkness

From Tablet 3, Verse 18.

O men, list to the voice of Wisdom;
list to the voice of Light.

Mysteries there are in the Cosmos
that unveiled fill the world with their Light.

Let he who would be free
from the bonds of darkness
first divine the material from the immaterial,
the fire from the earth;

for know ye that as earth descends to earth,
so also fire ascends unto fire
and becomes one with fire.

He who knows the fire that is within himself
shall ascend unto the eternal fire
and dwell in it eternally.

Thoth's Commentary, in Modern English:

The voice of Wisdom IS the voice of Light. It is in paying attention to your inner guidance, that the great mysteries of the cosmos are revealed.

If you desire to be free from the bonds of darkness... release all fears of being overtaken by that darkness.

First, realize that there is a difference between the material world and the spiritual world.

The fire within your soul... is related to the fire within the earth.
Your body will return to earth dust one day, but the fire in your soul will live on.

When you KNOW that the fire within your soul is eternal, then you do not fear death. Your soul is eternally one with the fire.

Seshat Contributes Her Wisdom:

While the material world is needed for man's existence on the Earth plane, it is his inner fire that lives on forever.

There must be a balance of the material and the immaterial (Fire of Spirit), to bring about the unveiling of even more mysteries.
Man has long sought after the unknown.

It is an unquenchable fire within, that keeps **US** ever evolving!

(Seshat uses the word **"US"** ... because every Deity figure is also seeking evolution. There is no stagnation in the human field... or the spiritual field.)

Chapter Nineteen

The Most Potent Fire of All

From Tablet 3, Verse 19.

Fire, the inner fire, is the most potent of all force,
for it overcometh all things
and penetrates to all things of the Earth.

Man supports himself only on that which resists.
So Earth must resist man else he existeth not.

Thoth's Commentary, in Modern English:

The Fire of the Soul is indeed the most potent force
in all of the Universe... for it is capable of overcoming
all obstacles.

There is no part of the Earth that this "human fire"
cannot penetrate.

There must be resistance, or opposite to what is
desired, to bring about appreciation. Light would not
be appreciated... if there was no dark.

Good would not even be recognized... if there was no evil. All forces contribute toward man's evolution.

Seshat Contributes Her Wisdom:

The inner fire is akin to the magnetism that is generated by the heart. Humanity's consciousness is a bridge, between the seen and the unseen.

It is the joining of these two elements that make it possible to transform all things.

Resistance is but a stepping stone to higher evolution. When one obstacle is dissolved, another takes its place. Overcoming and transforming... is the path of greatest evolution. This Earth plane is destined to always be on the cutting edge of evolutionary growth!

Other species gather around to watch as humanity struggles to move forward. You have a great cheer-leading section of benevolent beings. Be aware that there are also nefarious beings who wish you harm.

Remember that the Light always prevails!

Therefore my Beloved Thoth has always admonished humanity to seek the Light.

Chapter Twenty

Different Strokes for Different Folks

From Tablet 3, Verse 20.

All eyes do not see with the same vision,
for to one an object appears of one form and color and
appears different to the eye of another.

So also, the infinite fire,
changing from color to color,
is never the same from day to day.

Thoth's Commentary, in Modern English:

One hundred people can witness the same event…
yet there will be different perceptions by each
person.

This is because each person has their own filter
system, based on past and current circumstances of
their life.

The fire in the soul is constantly changing, as well. It moves in rapport with the communication of the heart's desire within.

An earthly flame flickers, waning and then growing again. So too, this inner fire illuminates with many different colors, according to the soul's purpose.

No two soul flames are ever alike at the same time, and should not be compared, one to another.

Seshat Contributes Her Wisdom:

Every individual is on their own path. Each person has their own purpose, according to agreements made before incarnation.

Some people spend lifetime after lifetime pursuing the same goal.
We respect the soul fire of each of you, and the purpose for which you came.

It is not profitable to compare your soul's journey to that of another. We all see with a different vision. Let all honor the vision of others.

Please cease to compare yourself with others. Your path is the only path that is best for you. Your journey is the only one that you are responsible for.

Chapter Twenty-one

Man's Fire Can Never be Quenched

From Tablet 3, Verse 21.

Thus, speak I, THOTH, of my Wisdom,
for man is a fire burning bright through the night;
never is quenched in the veil of the darkness,
never is quenched by the veil of the night.

Thoth's Commentary, in Modern English:

As I have observed through many lifetimes...
Man is indeed like a blazing fire that burns brightly, no
matter how strong the darkness.

The fire of the soul can never be quenched... for that
fire is eternal.

Seshat Contributes Her Wisdom:

Thoth seeks to let humanity know that the fire of the
soul can **never** be extinguished.

No matter what veils disguise the dark evil… **the Light will always prevail.**

This Earth will not see destruction... as long as man holds to the Light and BELIEVES that no darkness is more powerful than the Light of the soul.

Chapter Twenty-two

Freedom From The Bondage of Strife

From Tablet 3, Verse 22.

Into men's hearts, I looked by my Wisdom,
found them not free from the bondage of strife.

Free from the toils, thy fire, O my brother,
lest it be buried in the shadow of night!

Thoth's Commentary, in Modern English:

I have looked into the hearts of men, and sadly, have
seen that they still hold onto a mindset of bondage
and enslavement.

It is recognition of the power of the fire burning within,
that will cause a permanent change in this belief.

The fire within represents the Power of Divinity that
humanity possesses.
Acknowledging this power, will bring one into a place
of releasing the old chains of enslavement.

Man is not meant to toil so savagely!
There is a better way.

It all begins with realizing your VALUE as a Divine Being, filled with Holy Fire! If man never seeks to use this forgotten Power… he will surely be buried in the dark energy of ceaseless toil.

Seshat Contributes Her Wisdom:

My Beloved Thoth has always sought to be a teacher, and servant of mankind.

Despite Thoth's sharing so much Wisdom, there is still a pattern of enslavement and bondage to authority figures, among much of humanity.

Still, humans do not recognize that they are royalty!
A product of the stars!

Now, at this time, mankind is waking up as never before.
Pay attention to the fire within your heart and follow where it leads you.

Recognizing your own Divinity... is the best antidote to enslavement!

Chapter Twenty-three

Create Through Invisible Light

From Tablet 3, Verse 23.

Hark ye, O man, and list to this Wisdom:
where do name and form cease?

Only in consciousness, invisible,
an infinite force of radiance bright.

The forms that ye create
by brightening thy vision
are truly effects that follow thy cause.

Thoth's Commentary, in Modern English:

When does man cease to identify himself by only his
name and his physical body?

It is only in the Spirit mind or consciousness, that
man can create those things which he desires.

Expand your vision to express the Divinity that you are.

Seshat Contributes Her Wisdom:

Trying to create only from the physical realm, will not get you where you are longing to go.

Those things created with Light and Power from within, are the things beyond mere physical.

All things that are created in physical form, were first visioned in the mind and Spirit.

Yet, physical forms are required to sustain Life. Seek first your inner guidance, and bright will be the path before you.

You will find it far easier to attain all of your goals, by starting from the unconscious level.
Heed the callings of that bright flame in your heart.

Chapter Twenty-four

We Are Stardust

From Tablet 3, Verse 24.

Man is a star bound to a body,
until in the end, he is freed through his strife.

Only by struggle and toiling thy utmost
shall the star within thee bloom out in new life.

He who knows the commencement of all things,
free is his star from the realms of night.

Thoth's Commentary, in Modern English:

Mankind is composed of elements from the stars.
As he transitions from this earthly form, the star is
released.

In his life, he may struggle to attain awareness of the
Light within his own star.

As mankind realizes the progression of his evolution… he becomes aware of the Starlight within and is free from all darkness.
As he realizes that star-power was within him all along, so shall he ever be free, even in his physical lifetime!

Seshat Contributes Her Wisdom:

Humanity is comprised of the elements of space. Contributions from every star-species inhabit your DNA.

You presume that you must struggle and toil to attain the Light and yet… you already ARE the LIGHT!

As you become aware of the forward progression of all things… so too shall you embrace your own Light.

Exercise to Become Aware of Your Own Starlight:

Relax.
Imagine that you are in a void of darkness... far off among the stars.

Stillness is everywhere and peace is in your heart.
Look at the blue-black void around you.

See the twinkling stars of every color.
Hold aloft your arm.
See that it too is blue-black.

Look closely and see the reflection of the stars within
your own body.
Merge with the stars… feel them lighting up your
DNA responses.

Feel the spinal column fluid as it surges throughout
the nervous system, releasing this message:
We are star-royalty!
We are Light!

As we see our relation to the stars... we give our-
selves permission to grow stronger in this Light.
There is great value in contemplating the Light within
each cell.

This practice builds your power to create.

Have patience with the process.
Yes, perhaps it is a new thing for you… contemplating your own Starlight.

Yet, it is amazingly effective for awakening ancient
memories … which is why you are attracted to The
Emerald Tablets in the first place.

Knowing that YOU are Starlight will help you to
remember who you are.

Chapter Twenty-five

Everything in the Universe Changes

From Tablet 3, Verse 25.

Remember, O man, that all which exists
is only another form of that which exists not.
Everything that has being
is passing into yet other being
and thou thyself are not an exception.

Thoth's Commentary, in Modern English:

Everything that IS... has been in another form at one time.

All that IS NOW... is currently passing into another form.

All matter and non-matter are forms of energy.
Energy simply changes its composition and vibratory rate.

You and your physical body and mind are constantly changing with time.

One day, you will leave physical form to be one with the Earth.

Seshat Contributes Her Wisdom:

All is created by thought first. So anything created by man, was once a thought.

In nature, a seed becomes a tree, a cloud turns into rain, a stream emerges as a mighty river… all is constantly changing!

Humanity is constantly changing... even when you think that you are staying still. This continual change is referred to by one of the immutable laws of the Universe -

The Law of Perpetual Transmutation of Energy:

Everything is constantly changing. Some changes are not noticed, as they are occurring at cellular or atomic levels… but they ARE changing, nonetheless.

Chapter Twenty-six

Don't Go Breaking the Law!

From Tablet 3, Verse 26.

Consider the Law, for all is Law.
Seek not that which is not of the Law,
for such exists only in the illusions of the senses.

Thoth's Commentary, in Modern English:

There is a Universal Law that applies to every situation and every being. It is only an illusion... to think that the Universal Laws do not apply to you. When you try to go against Natural Law, it is only an imaginary quest with no substance.

Seshat Contributes Her Wisdom:

Ponder the Laws of the Universe, when making decisions about your life. There is no need to search a law book... for the Laws that govern humanity are already written on the walls of your heart.

As We have said time and time again… follow the Wisdom that you already know to be true.

It is easy when you go within and heed the promptings of your own soul.

Chapter Twenty-seven

Wisdom Comes to All Who Seek

From Tablet 3, Verse 27.

Wisdom cometh to all her children
even as they cometh unto wisdom.

Thoth's Commentary, in Modern English:

As you seek Wisdom, Wisdom is seeking you. Wisdom is eager to find a home within YOU!

Seshat Contributes Her Wisdom:

I refer again to the Laws of the Universe.

The Law of Attraction - that which is like unto itself... is drawn to itself.

Or, even more plainly - like attracts like.
Wisdom is seeking the seeker... even as the seeker, is seeking Wisdom!

Chapter Twenty-eight

Hidden Mysteries

From Tablet 3, Verse 28.

All through the ages, the Light has been hidden.
Awake, O man, and be wise.
Deep in the mysteries of life have I traveled,
seeking and searching for that which is hidden.
List ye, O man, and be wise.

Thoth's Commentary, in Modern English:

Throughout all time, Light has been something to search for.

Listen to my words of Wisdom. That which is most valuable... must be sought after.

I have traveled through many Dimensions, seeking out the mysteries, far too enormous to put into this small text.

Yet, as you seek Wisdom and follow your guidance, you too, shall be wise and see greater mysteries.

Seshat Contributes Her Wisdom:

You have the capacity to take in the Light, through the magnificence of your heart, and its magnetic field.

This is one of the greatest hidden mysteries of all. For after traveling throughout the cosmos, my Beloved Thoth stated that he found no greater mystery, than that found in the heart of man.

Referring to: Tablet 1, Verse 15 of the Original Emerald Tablets

Free was I of the Halls of Amenti,
bound not by death to the circle of life.
Far to the stars I journeyed
until space and time became as naught.

Then having drunk deep of the cup of Wisdom,
I looked into the hearts of men
and there found I greater mysteries and was glad.

For only in the Search for Truth
could my Soul be stilled
and the flame within be quenched.

Tablet 1, Verse 15 as quoted from:
Study Edition: The Emerald Tablets of Thoth The Atlantean - Available from Amazon, Barnes and Noble, and Other Fine Bookstores.

Chapter Twenty-nine

Man's Heart is Full of Light

From Tablet 3, Verse 29.

Far 'neath the Earth crust, in the Halls of Amenti,
mysteries I saw that are hidden from men.

Oft have I journeyed the deep hidden passage,
looked on the Light that is Life among men.
There 'neath the Flowers of Life ever living,
searched I the hearts and the secrets of men.
Found I that man is but living in darkness,
Light of the Great Fire is hidden within.

Thoth's Commentary, in Modern English:

The Halls of Amenti lie deep beneath the Earth's
crust.

I traveled there many times, and looked upon the
Flower of Life, that gives and sustains life.

There I searched and contemplated the hearts of
man.

I found that man does not recognize his own Great Fire, as it is hidden within.

Seshat Contributes Her Wisdom:

Again, Thoth, my Beloved, is speaking of the hearts of man. Although he lived many lifetimes and traveled to the halls of Amenti each time… he still found that man does not recognize the capacity for Light that is already within him.

Chapter Thirty

The Seven Lords of the Frequencies

From Tablet 3, Verse 30.

Before the Lords of hidden Amenti
learned I the Wisdom I give unto men.
Masters are they of the great Secret Wisdom,
brought from the future of infinity's end.
Seven are they, the Lords of Amenti,
overlords they of the Children of Morning,
Suns of the cycles, Masters of Wisdom.

Formed are not they as the children of men?
THREE, FOUR, FIVE AND SIX, SEVEN, EIGHT,
NINE
are the Titles of the Masters of men.

Thoth's Commentary, in Modern English:

It was from the Lords of hidden Amenti (a place of
power and renewal) that I, Thoth, learned of many
mysteries.

The Seven Lords are Masters of great Wisdom, Overlords of the Children of Morning, Suns of the Cycles… they are Masters of Wisdom.

These Seven Overlords are not formed as men but are composed of Frequencies of Light and Vibration.

Three, Four, Five and Six, Seven, Eight and Nine are the Titles of these Masters. They govern and rule over the various Dimensions.

Their Names and Frequencies are:

Untanas - (Three) - Third Dimension
Quertas - (Four) - Fourth Dimension
Chietal - (Five) - Fifth Dimension
Goyana - (Six) - Sixth Dimension
Huertal - (Seven) - Seventh Dimension
SemVeta - (Eight) - Eighth Dimension
Ardal - (Nine) - Ninth Dimension

These numbers and names represent the Dimensions and powerful Frequencies therein.

This is why the numbers begin with Three instead of One. Three is the Third Dimension, with its own Frequency.

Each of the Seven Lords has their own Frequency, yet they work together as One Unit… in their capacity to rule the Spheres and Dimensions.

Seshat Contributes Her Wisdom:

Having a panel of Overlords, each with his own
Power, yet, working together as a whole, ensures
fairness and equal powers in all of the Dimensions.

You may call upon one or all these Frequency Lords
to be of assistance to you.
They relate also to the human Chakra System.

Untanas - (Three) - Crown Chakra
Quertas - (Four) - Third Eye Chakra
Chietal - (Five) - Throat Chakra
Goyana - (Six) - Heart Chakra
Huertal - (Seven) - Solar Plexus Chakra
SemVeta - (Eight) - Sexual Chakra
Ardal - (Nine) - Root Chakra

It is greatly beneficial to touch each of your Chakras
while repeating the names of the specific Lord.

Chapter Thirty-one

Back From the Future

From Tablet 3, Verse 31.

Far from the future, formless yet forming,
came they as teachers for the children of men.
Live they forever, yet not of the living,
bound not to life and yet free from death.

Rule they forever with infinite wisdom,
bound yet not bound to the dark Halls of Death.
Life they have in them, yet life that is not life,
free from all are the Lords of the ALL.

Thoth's Commentary, in Modern English:

These Seven Lords have come back in time from the future... to teach us.

Because they are Pure Frequencies, they cannot die as we know death.

They rule the Dimensions forever with Infinite Wisdom.

It is their choice, acting as a bond, that keeps them as teachers of man.

Yes, they do have Life, but not Life as we experience it.

They are completely free of all Dimensional ties, yet they choose to stay, to be a balance for all of humanity.

Seshat Contributes Her Wisdom:

Simply knowing the names of the Seven Lords of Frequencies, is a valuable tool.

As you call upon their names, the Frequencies they govern begin to vibrate within your own bodies. There is much about you... that is in the realm of the unseen.

Becoming more aware of your Frequency State at each moment, is a sign of your evolution. You need not understand it with your logical mind.

Be open to understanding... and more will come to you.

The Seven Lords came back to you from the future... to teach you in the ways of Frequency and Light. Call upon them often for help in adjusting your frequencies to higher and higher realms.

Relax and let this be easy.

Do not fret and overanalyze. But question... always question. It is a poor teacher who does not encourage his students to ask questions.

Have patience, and knowledge will be awakened within your heart. TRUST that your heart will always guide you to Truth!

Chapter Thirty-two

The LOGOS

From Tablet 3, Verse 32.

Forth from them, came forth the LOGOS,
instruments they of the Power o'er all.
Vast is their countenance,
yet hidden in smallness,
formed by a forming,
known yet unknown.

Thoth's Commentary, in Modern English:

From the Seven Lords of Frequencies came forth the
Principles of Divine Reason and Creative Order.
These Lords of Frequency are instruments of Power
over all things in this and other Dimensions.

Although they are great, it is only as one seeks them
in the stillness of the heart, that they may be found.

They sometimes take on forms of existence as needed.
Yet, much unknown Wisdom is still to be revealed.

Seshat Contributes Her Wisdom:

Divine Reason, Creative Order, and the Law are as ONE.

Yes, these Lords have great Power, yet they hide it in the very place in which one would not think to look.

Within each human is a set of genetic materials, that can be activated by reciting the name of the Lords and calling forth their Power.

This is an incorruptible power that CANNOT be used for evil.

The Law of Vibration is alive in them... as it is alive in YOU!

The Law of Vibration -

All particles of all substances are in constant movement.

The Lords may appear as human for a cause. Their vibrations are always in movement, even as they may appear to be still.

Chapter Thirty-three

Frequency Lord Untanas/THREE

From Tablet 3, Verse 33.

THREE holds the Key of all Hidden Magic,
creator He of the Halls of the Dead;
sending forth power, shrouding with darkness,
binding the souls of the children of men;
sending the darkness, binding the soul force;
director of negative to the children of men.

Thoth's Commentary, in Modern English:

The Lord THREE or Untanas, holds the Key of Hidden Magic for this Dimension. For humanity is still in the Third Dimension.

Lord Untanas is associated with the Crown Chakra.

Yes, Untanas created the Halls of the Dead, which refers to a place of resting and rejuvenation. This is NOT a hellish realm as some suppose. This is referring to the place between lives… or the "Other Side."

He may also be referred to as The Angel of Death. Yet, fear not the Angel of Death, for He takes you safely to a place of rest. You will always be reincarnating until you evolve to a place of knowledge.

This is the Hidden Magic, realizing that you can request all THIS lifetime's memories to be brought forward into the next.

Seshat Contributes Her Wisdom:

You can request to spend your next lifetime on a planet of your choosing. This is also a Hidden Magic. Take more care when choosing the next lifetime, and what you desire to experience therein.

Many are so hungry for growth that they forget to give themselves a lifetime of ease somewhere. The Earth plane is one of the most difficult of all of the realms.
Choosing too many difficult lifetimes in a row, can cause burnout quickly. This is one reason many Light-workers today feel like giving up.

Chapter Thirty-four

Frequency Lord QUERTAS/FOUR

From Tablet 3, Verse 34.

FOUR is He who looses the Power.
Lord, He, of Life to the children of men.
Light is his body; flame is his countenance.
freer of souls to the children of men.

Thoth's Commentary, in Modern English:

Quertas is Lord of the Fourth Realm. He is associated with the Third Eye Chakra. In almost every plane of existence there is a "savior figure."

In Christianity, this is the Christ.
In Buddhism, this is the Buddha (of which there are many).
In Islam this is the prophet Mohammed.
In many religions, there are "savior figures."

All "savior figures" have one aspect in common… they set free the souls of the men and women who believe in them.

Seshat Contributes Her Wisdom:

Thoth has spoken well on the Fourth Lord.
I would add this…
There are many humans who act as "savior figures"
for the good of mankind. They are often raised up to
the position of Sainthood. This is an example of how
one can evolve in giant steps here on this planet.

However, please note that many of these "savior
figures," who attained Sainthood, suffered greatly
in their lifetime. Often it was not until long after their
death, that their gift to humanity was recognized.

A mistake occurs when one takes on TOO much
responsibility for the growth of others, and feels it is
their DUTY to save them from their journey.

It is important to always respect the "soul plan" of
another. You may think you KNOW for sure what is
good for someone else, and fight to make them over
into your mold.

Keep your eyes steadfastly upon your own soul's
journey.

Chapter Thirty-five

Frequency Lord Chietal/FIVE

From Tablet 3, Verse 35.

FIVE is the Master, the Lord of all Magic -
Key to The Word that resounds among men.

Thoth's Commentary, in Modern English:

Cheital is indeed the Lord of all Magic, for He is
associated with the Throat Chakra!

Speak the WORDS that resound among men...
with the Power of your voice! This is a seat of
Power that is most often overlooked by those
seeking a spiritual path.

So eager are you to be humble, that often you do not
speak your own Truth.

Call upon the Power of this great Lord, Chietal, to
help you to find your own true Power!

Seshat Contributes Her Wisdom:

What Magic could you create if you felt free to speak up more often?

What Magic could you create if you asked for what you really wanted in life, instead of settling for less?

Not speaking out your desires, or even voicing your thoughts, comes from old programming of unworthiness!

As you release the bondage of your Throat Chakra, you will find yourself expecting more, and receiving more of what you desire in your heart.

An exceptionally good exercise to open your Throat Chakra is to chant Cheital several times daily...**very loudly!**
Then switch to chanting His Name several times **very softly**.
Play with this exercise until it becomes fun for you.

Each time you call upon the name of this Lord...your own Power grows stronger!

An Exercise to Manifest Your Desires:

Switch the focus to YOUR desires and shout them out as commands to the Universe!
Try it…

I DESIRE and EXPECT to RECEIVE (insert your desire).

Play with all the ways that you can use your voice in this exercise.
Be sure to RESIST any temptation to whine or justify WHY you have the desire.

You are WORTHY to desire anything WITHOUT having to explain to any Deity or person WHY you desire it!
Get accustomed to hearing your own voice speaking your desires out loud.

Chapter Thirty-six

Frequency Lord Goyana/SIX

From Tablet 3, Verse 36.

SIX is the Lord of Light, the hidden pathway,
path of the souls of the children of men.

Thoth's Commentary, in Modern English:

SIX, Lord of Light, indeed... for His Name is Goyana
and He is associated with the Heart Chakra.

The heart IS the hidden pathway that so many ignore
for the greatness it holds!

The path of the heart... is the path of your Life. All
that you need to know is already written there, on the
walls of your heart. Be still, go within, search your
heart in the stillness, and that hidden pathway will be
revealed to you.

Seshat Contributes Her Wisdom:

In all of this teaching, we have been speaking over and over about the Wisdom of the heart.
The desires of your heart are your guidelines to your soul purpose.

Call upon Lord Goyana to help you to open up your heart to the Wisdom that is already there!
True Beings of Light will always point you in the direction of your heart.

Chapter Thirty-seven

Frequency Lord Huertal/SEVEN

From Tablet 3, Verse 37.

SEVEN is He who is Lord of the Vastness,
Master of Space and the Key of the Times.

Thoth's Commentary, in Modern English:

Huertal is Lord of the Solar Plexus Chakra!
Herein you find the will of man.

This Lord is the Master of all Space and holds the
Keys of Time.
The human will is the master of all space and time...
whether man is aware of this or not.

Seshat Contributes Her Wisdom:

Much good will come as you focus on strengthening
the Solar Plexus Chakra.
Only YOU... are in charge of YOU.

As you grow in confidence that your will CAN be strengthened, so shall more and more good come to you.

It is very discouraging to your spiritual growth, to feel as if someone or something ELSE is in charge of you!

Perhaps, in times past, you have given up your Power. It is now time to take back **ALL** the Power that you have mistakenly given to others.

Begin by focusing on your will.
Avoid giving attention to all the times in which you failed at using your will (ex. in a weight loss effort).

Yes, acknowledge briefly past incidents... yet do not stay there.
It does not matter what has gone before. NOW is the time to claim your own will, and the Power that you have to use that power!

This Lord, or Frequency, can help you to raise your own awareness.
The Solar Plexus is His domain, and He seeks to be of service.
Huertal, Huertal, Huertal!

And remember, you are NOT in servitude to Huertal! His mission is to be of service to all.

Do these Lords of Frequencies a favor… Help a Lord fulfill His mission!

P.S.: In the original Tablets, Thoth, My Beloved, did refer to these Frequencies as Lords. The Lords are interchangeably masculine or feminine.
Whatever makes you feel more comfortable… use that gender. In truth, these **Sound Frequencies activate a sound signature that is genderless.**

Simply chanting the Names, corresponds to the Frequencies within you, that are already there. You simply activate MORE by using the Power of these Frequencies.

Chapter Thirty-eight

Frequency Lord SemVeta/EIGHT

From Tablet 3, Verse 38.

EIGHT is He who orders the progress;
weighs and balances the journey of men.

Thoth's Commentary, in Modern English:

EIGHT is the Lord or Governor of the Sexual Chakra.
This is the center of creation for both male and
female.

His name is SemVeta. Of course, the Sexual Chakra
weighs and balances the evolution and progress of
all of humanity. Not only human life, but animal, plant,
and even elemental lives, are ruled by the Power of
creation.

Nature itself brings a balance of evolution to all species.

Many Light Workers are a bit ashamed of the Sexual
Chakra, yet without a healthy Sex Chakra... all the

other energy vortexes are cut off with barely a trickle of Life.

Indeed, the BALANCE of the journey of all creation is found within the Sexual Chakra!

Seshat Contributes Her Wisdom:

SemVeta, SemVeta, SemVeta! I can hear it now…
ringing out from bedrooms across the globe!
Who knew that a Sound Frequency could activate
this often-ignored Chakra?

I will give practical uses for this activation...

Chanting the name SemVeta, calls more energy into
any creative endeavor.
Try it and you will see!

This Sound Frequency will be extremely helpful in
all areas of sexuality. Men can use the Frequency to
help with stimulation of blood flow, that is essential to
having a firm erection.

Women can use the Frequency, SemVeta, to
increase desire and moisten the vaginal area.
What?
Are you shocked?

As the author often says… "Spiritual information is of no value, if it cannot be used to improve human life." I, Seshat, do agree wholeheartedly!

You are a spiritual being experiencing a human lifetime.
Take all the pleasure that you can.

If information that you are studying does not help you in a practical way… look elsewhere.

Chapter Thirty-nine

Frequency Lord Ardal/NINE

From Tablet 3, Verse 39.

NINE is the Father, vast He of countenance,
forming and changing from out of the formless.

Thoth's Commentary, in Modern English:

In the beginning was the Root Chakra.
Ardal is the Name and Frequency of this Lord.
All your connections to all of life, spring from this
Chakra.

Yes, your ancient origins still influence you in many
ways.
Recognizing that this Sound Frequency of ARDAL
has the power to change some of the old slave men-
tality... is one Key to evolution.

Seshat Contributes Her Wisdom:

To use the power of this Lord's Frequency to positively influence your Root Chakra… Do this:

Place your hand on your Root Chakra. Ask your OWN Inner Guidance what needs to be shifted in your primal roots.

Be still and do not stress if you feel nothing.
Your Root Chakra can hold a lot of secrets.
Begin to chant the name of ARDAL!
Feel how that Sound reverberates within your being.
Let this be easy.

Each time you call upon ANY of these Frequencies, the Power is cumulative.
Remember, it took eons for your Root Chakra to accumulate all of the information that it now holds.

Concentrating on clearing ONE thing at a time is best.
Or simply place your hand on the Root Chakra, chant the Name or Sound Frequency, Ardal… and ask for the highest good for all!
Moving forward does not have to be difficult!

Chapter Forty

Hidden Keys

From Tablet 3, Verse 40.

Meditate on the symbols I give thee.
Keys are they, though hidden from men.

Thoth's Commentary, in Modern English:

As you read my original text from Emerald Tablet
Three… relax and take the words into your heart.
Yes, there are many keys hidden therein. You would
not be attracted to this information if you had not
had some type of association with me in a previous
incarnation.

If you decide to "let this be easy" and do not stress
that you do NOT understand it all yet… Light will
come upon you.
There is no hurry, all is well. You chose to be in the
exact place that you are now.

Seshat Contributes Her Wisdom:

You may be curious as to exactly what these KEYS are.

One set of Keys, we have already given you… seek after that which your heart desires.

As you do this ONE thing… much more will be revealed to you.

Are you willing to accept that spiritual growth could be as easy as going within, and paying attention to what your heart tells you?

Chapter Forty-one

Using the Frequency Keys

From Tablet 3, Verse 41.

Reach ever upward, O Soul of the morning.
Turn thy thoughts upward to Light and to Life.
Find in the Keys of the numbers I bring thee,
Light on the pathway from Life unto Life.

Thoth's Commentary, in Modern English:

Keep reaching upwards in your quest for deeper
understanding.
Bring your thoughts always back to the positive
vibrations.

Use the Frequencies of the Seven Lords that I have
given to you. Recite all of the Names daily as you
touch each Chakra point.

You will find much Light on the path, as it becomes
easier and easier for you to understand Light and
Truth.

Seshat Contributes Her Wisdom:

As a woman, I find these exercises to be greatly beneficial for humans of every gender. You all have an energy system... a Chakra system, that can benefit from the vibrations created by chanting the Names of the Seven Lords.
It is easy to remember as:

Untanas starts at the Crown Chakra, and opens you to Spiritual Wisdom.

Quertas activates the Pineal gland. This increases your inner vision and ability to receive and transmit psychic information.

Cheital activates the Throat Chakra, encouraging you to speak up and speak out.

Powerful Goyana vibrates the Heart, and opens you to more love, understanding, and courage to follow your heart's desires.

Huertal coincides with the Solar Plexus, seat of your will, and the powerful "GUT FEELING"!

SemVeta stimulates the Sexual Chakra...and all of the good feelings that are generated there!

Ardal brings it all together by addressing your primal needs, primal roots, thus stimulating hunger for more than mere survival.

You will find your life much more in harmony with what YOU want, as you cultivate the habit of daily balance.

If spiritual growth is your quest… this is a very great Key to assist you. In all of your desires for spiritual growth, do not forget the joys of being human.

Chapter Forty-two

The Flower of Light IS Life

From Tablet 3, Verse 42.

Seek ye with Wisdom. Turn thy thoughts inward.
Close not thy mind to the Flower of Light.

Thoth's Commentary, in Modern English:

Take your time and use your inner Wisdom. Look
within for the guidance that you already have within
you. Keep your heart and mind open to the Flower of
Light.

**Flower of Light meditation free audio at:
rebeccamarina.com/resources (Listening
Recommended)**

Seshat Contributes Her Wisdom:

We have spoken often of the power within your
heart. The Flower of Light refers to the Divine Flame
that is in every being.

Some refer to this flame as the Flame of the Holy Spirit.

Without this flame, by whatever name you desire to call it… there is no Life.
The flame animates ALL Life from plant, to animal, to human.
When you see a dead body of any species, you can tell right away that there is no animating Spirit within.

Be wise, be still, and listen. Then, when it is time for inspired action… you will KNOW what to do.

Chapter Forty-three

How to Manifest Your Heart's Desires

From Tablet 3, Verse 43.

Place in thy body a thought-formed picture.
Think of the numbers that lead thee to Life.

Thoth's Commentary, in Modern English:

Picture in your mind what it is that you desire. Focus also, on how each energy center or chakra, has a part in delivering that to you.
The numbers coincide with the Lords of Frequency.

Everything is Frequency. All can be reached in your quest for more Life!

Seshat Contributes Her Wisdom:

Your body has its own Wisdom, it knows what is best for it, and it knows what is best avoided.
As you hold a firm picture of that which you desire and really FEEL it in your body… so shall it more easily manifest for you.

Chapter Forty-four

Seeking Wisdom

From Tablet 3, Verse 44.

Clear is the pathway to he who has Wisdom.
Open the door to the Kingdom of Light.

Thoth's Commentary, in Modern English:

As you take the time to study these teachings, you
will become wiser. This will keep you from acting
hastily and making many mistakes.

Wisdom comes from study. However, Wisdom also
comes from life experience. Save time and learn
from others who have gone before you.

Seshat Contributes Her Wisdom:

There have been many wonderful teachers who have
gone before you. All have made mistakes in using
Wisdom... Let not your heart be discouraged, as you
look upon the mistakes which YOU have made.

Place LIGHT on the mistakes and thank them for teaching you. Easy is the path to those who pay attention, judge not, and forgive often!

Chapter Forty-five

Your Powerful Flame is Awareness

From Tablet 3, Verse 45.

Pour forth thy flame as a Sun of the morning.
Shut out the darkness and live in the day.

Thoth's Commentary, in Modern English:

There is a flame within your being that can never be
quenched!
You have far more Power than you know.
Shut out those dark energies who would try to cor-
rupt the flame of your heart.
Live in the Light by choosing the Good every time.

Seshat Contributes Her Wisdom:

A good way to know that you are basking in
the Light, is to check in with your thoughts and
conversations.
Do you recognize when you are in judgment of others?
It is simple to turn this around.

Awareness is key.

Do your thoughts feel uplifting to you?
If not, what could make them so?
Be aware that you are the Master of your own being,
of your own growth.
You DO HAVE THE POWER to choose LIGHT!

Chapter Forty-six

Follow the Path of Thoth

From Tablet 3, Verse 46.

Take thee, O man, as part of thy being,
the Seven who are, but are not as they seem.
Opened, O man, have I my Wisdom.
Follow the path in the way I have led.

Thoth's Commentary, in Modern English:

Take the Power and assistance which these Seven
Lords of Frequency are offering to you.

Follow this guidance, activate your own chakras with
the power of these Sound Frequencies… and you
shall see great advancement in your soul.
Follow this path and more shall be revealed to you!

Seshat Contributes Her Wisdom:

Remember that Goyana is the center connecting
point of all of the Chakras. The heart is eager to
know all that will cause you growth.

The Seven are surely NOT as they seem, for they seemed to be such a mystery, did they not?
Yet, looking at the assistance that their Frequencies can give to your body's entire energy system, is a precious treasure.

The Frequency of Lord Goyana sends energy upwards to the Throat, Third Eye, and Crown Chakras.

Beating in rhythm to your heart's desires (if you are paying attention to them) Goyana sends energy downward to the Solar Plexus, Sexual and Root Chakras.

Focusing on the Heart Chakra, is a blessing to your entire being!

Chapter Forty-seven

The Light Path to True Wisdom

From Tablet 3, Verse 47.

Masters of Wisdom,
SUN of the MORNING
LIGHT and LIFE to the children of men.

Thoth's Commentary, in Modern English:

WE have given you a Light to follow. Your Chakra system holds many secrets. You shall become Masters of Wisdom!
You shall be as a Light unto the children of men.
Hold fast to your heart's callings. Always turn your thoughts back to the Light.

Seshat Contributes Her Wisdom:

Spend time in the stillness... holding thoughts of fulfilling your heart's desires.
When dark thoughts would overtake you, turn to your Divinity within. Call upon the Divine Figures whom

you look up to, when you feel that you need extra guidance or protection.

Be it Jesus the Christ, Lakshmi, Quan Yin, Zeus, Allah, or any other Being of Light...
All desire to be of service to humanity, or they would not BE a BEING of LIGHT!

There is ONE Source. Yet from that One Source, flow multiple streams of helping energies.

Your LIGHT among men, is surely found in that great fountain of Light within your heart.

Do not diminish the power which you ALREADY have to be a Light among men!

Do as your heart guides you, and it shall be so.

Chapter Forty-eight

Preparations for Channeling

Please have a notebook handy to do this work. You may want to do these fun exercises many times over. It is nice to have all the exercises in one place, so that you can see how wonderfully you are coming along!

Before you begin:
Here is a question that ALWAYS comes up when I am teaching a class on Channeling.

Question: What if I attract a Dark being? How do I know if this is a Being of Light?

Answer: Simple... you INTEND to attract ONLY Beings of 100% PURE LIGHT! Say it out loud!
I intend to attract ONLY Beings of 100% PURE GOD-LIGHT!

If you have any doubts, you ASK the Being... Are you 100% PURE GOD-LIGHT?

You ask three times...
They CANNOT LIE! It is LAW!

Remember, YOU are a Being of tremendous spiritual authority. Know it, Feel it, Use it!

Here are the Basic Instructions for Channeling ANY Being of Light... using the dominant/non-dominant handwriting method:

It is easy and natural to Channel, if you allow yourself to relax, and do not be too concerned about getting it perfect at first.
I have taught hundreds of people to Channel. They were all pleasantly surprised at how easy it was from the very beginning.

It is important to allow yourself to take baby steps. Even the most famous Channel of this century, Esther Hicks, (who Channels Abraham) began very simply.

Esther states that in the very beginning, she wrote words in the air with her nose. She did not become discouraged and kept at the practice.
Now, Esther has Channeled the group of Spirit Teachers known as Abraham, for thousands of people around the world.

Beings of Light use Channeling to transmit Wisdom from Heavenly Realms into the third dimension.

Beings of Light are very eager to transmit their Wisdom, Love and Support. Yet, they need a human to be the voice. Let us begin by helping you to find and use your beautiful voice.

It's important to establish why you desire to Channel, whether it is Thoth, or ANY Being of Light!

Are you seeking specific information?

Are you seeking to transmit messages for the benefit of others?

Are you seeking to do this just for fun?

All reasons are valid, good and no cause for shame or embarrassment.

Would you like to know what every Light Being **wants from you?**

First and foremost, Light Beings want a **relationship with you**, **more** than they want anything else. This is why I recommend that you begin to Channel by establishing a relationship with the Light Being.

After all, would you like it if someone just wanted to ask you all kinds of questions, without even getting to know you? That would be very awkward. So always begin by establishing a relationship with any Being whom you wish to Channel.

For Thoth... I suggest that you write a greeting to Thoth, with your dominant hand, which could possibly say … Dear Thoth, I desire to form a relationship with you. Is that okay?

Now switch the pen into your non-dominant hand, and just be still for a moment. You will get one or two words in response, as all spiritual information comes through the right side of the brain.

Your Non-dominant hand is HARDWIRED to the right side of your brain. **Being right or left-handed does NOT affect this phenomenon.** Spiritual Information will ALWAYS come through the right side of your brain first.

(See FULL Instructions below)

It is very important that you actually write out the question, because there is Magic in the switching. When you are writing with your dominant hand, and then switch to your non-dominant hand for a response, **something special happens within your brain.**

You are creating **New Neural Pathways** between the right hemisphere of the brain and the left hemisphere of the brain. Information is transmitted via the Corpus Callosum, which is the thick bundle of nerves separating and connecting the right and left hemispheres of the brain.

Each time you do this exercise, you are creating more Neural Pathways. Soon, what seemed like a dim narrow path, will become a bright superhighway! With practice, you can receive Channeled information easily.

The great Light Being, Sanat Kumara, told me in a Channeling session, that the Corpus Callosum is a marvelous map system! This Sensitive Bundle of Nerves already contains a route for every Being of Light whom you may ever desire to Channel.

As you continue to do this exercise, writing a question with the dominant hand, and then switching the pen to answer with the non-dominant hand... you create more new Neural Pathways. Then information begins to flow very easily and rapidly.

I have been Channeling for many years, and yet, whenever I meet a new Being of Light, who desires for me to Channel information for them... I always take a few days to do dominant/non-dominant handwriting with them.

This increases the ease of communication exponentially!

It's important to start out with baby step questions. As I said earlier, establishing a relationship is KEY.

Below are some questions which I suggest that you use to start. Remember, it's very important to write out the question... even though I've written it for you... and **then** switch to the non-dominant hand to receive the answer.

Remember, this information will come through the right side of your brain. You **will not be possessed by some Spirit** that comes in to move your hand! There is a field of study called "automatic writing" - **this is not that study**.

You are not possessed... however, the information does flow into the right side of your brain... perhaps one tiny word at a time.

It's important to be gentle with yourself. Resist the impulse to be impatient. Just take this one baby step at a time.
Also, be cautious of the questions you decide to ask.

DO NOT be asking fortune-telling questions...

Question: What is a "fortune telling" question?

Answer: A question that demands that the Light Being foretell the future. Not even God has dominion over the FREE WILL of man.

There are always humans involved in every decision... and every single one of them has FREE WILL. Therefore, it is impossible for any being to accurately predict the future every time. It **IS possible** to make a prediction "based on the energy as it appears now."

Examples of "fortune telling" questions are:

- **When will my true love come**? He or she has FREE WILL... and you CANNOT impose your will on theirs.
- **When will this situation be resolved?** Again, other people and their FREE WILL are involved.
- **If I play these numbers in the lottery... will I win?**

Oh PLEASE! If you want to Channel ONLY for these reasons, you will NOT attract a Light Being with service to humanity in mind!

Better questions are: HOW can I accomplish something or... WHAT action can I take toward my goal?

Example:

- HOW can I get ready to attract my true love?
- WHAT can I DO to resolve this situation?
- WHAT can I DO to win big in life?

Do you see the difference in the questions?

Remember that Beings of Light are looking for relationship and partnership. When you ask HOW or WHAT... you are taking responsibility for **your part.**

One good resource for getting a general idea about your life CAN BE… but is not always - Astrology. Not the kind in the free column online, serious Astrology. I follow VEDIC Astrology myself - you follow your heart.

Even THEN… use Astrology only as a guideline, and don't agonize over it. To my way of thinking, we are given information, so that we can ask for guidance on how to CHANGE the things that we don't like!

You can also consult with a reliable psychic. Just remember... a psychic can only read the POSSIBILITIES of the energies, as they are showing at the time of your inquiry.

Back to Channeling:

Remember that Thoth (or ANY Light Being) desires to be of service to humanity... not your puppet! Also, remember what I said earlier, about being a friend and establishing a relationship. You would not be happy if someone only liked you because of the information that you could give them, would you? Keep that in mind as you begin this exercise.

It is important that you bring your Polarities into Balance as you begin this exercise. Here is a simple way to do that...

How to Balance your Polarities:

Tap gently on your Crown chakra, and say, Polarities Balance... Polarities Balance.

Tap gently on your Third eye, and say, Polarities Balance.

Tap gently on your Throat chakra, and say, Polarities Balance.

Tap gently on your Heart center, and say, Polarities Balance.

Tap gently on your Solar Plexus chakra, and say, Polarities Balance.

Tap gently on your Root chakra and say, Polarities Balance.

Take three breaths softly in and out...
Relax.

Roll your eyeballs gently upward towards your Third Eye. Do this three times. This helps you to move quickly into the Alpha Brainwave state… which is excellent for Channeling.

Chapter Forty-nine

Beginner Mini-Course in
Channeling Thoth

Now you are ready to begin:

Put your pen into your dominant hand and write out one of these questions.
It is IMPORTANT to write the question with your dominant hand (even though I just wrote it FOR you). There is MAGIC in the actual SWITCHING of your hands! **Do not cheat yourself of this Magic.**

With your dominant hand, write… **Dear Thoth, I would like to establish a relationship with you. Is there anything that you would like to say to me now?**

Write the question here:

_____

_____

_____

_____

Switch the pen now and allow information to flow to you… one word at a time. Remember that no Spirit is going to come to move your hand! The Wisdom is coming from Thoth… through the right side of your brain.

Write the response here. Give yourself plenty of room... as you will write big and sloppy. (Notice that the spacing is extra roomy.)

Write Thoth's response here:

_____

_____

_____

_____

_____

_____

After you have done that part of the exercise... move to another question. Put your pen back into your dominant hand, and write this... **Dear Thoth, is there anything that I can do for you?**

Write the question here:

_____

_____

_____

_____

_____

_____

Switch the pen back into your non-dominant hand and allow the Wisdom to flow... one little word at a time.

Write Thoth's response here:

_____

_____

_____

_____

_____

_____

I suggest that you repeat these two questions daily, until you begin to feel that the information is flowing more easily.

Expect that you are going to write big and sloppy, with the non-dominant hand. **That is perfectly right and good.**

It's important NOT to criticize yourself. And it's important NOT to be concerned that nobody could read this. Nobody else is supposed to read this... except for you. This is your exercise, for your spiritual growth.

This is JUST THE BEGINNING of your relationship with Thoth. It is up to you to continue and formulate more questions until the information flows more smoothly. As you progress, you may find that you do not need to ask questions at all. Just sit with pen in hand... and invite Thoth to come to you.

You may desire to have more Light on what you have received. Simply repeat the handwriting process asking:

- Will you please give me more clarity on what you said?
- What can I do to communicate with you more effectively?
- Do you see any spiritual or mental blocks? Please let me know what I can do to release/ heal them.

I would love to hear some of your experiences with this... so please drop me a line to tell me how you're doing:

Rebecca@Rebeccamarina.com

Chapter Fifty

Beginner Mini-Course in
Channeling Seshat

Follow the above basic instructions for Channeling through the use of dominant/non-dominant handwriting.

Be sure to Balance your Polarities first!

Put your pen into your dominant hand. Write out one of these questions...

It is IMPORTANT to write the question with your dominant hand (even though I just wrote it FOR you). There is MAGIC in the actual SWITCHING of your hands! **Do not cheat yourself of this Magic.**

With your dominant hand write... **Dear Seshat, I would like to establish a relationship with you. Is there anything that you would like to say to me now?**

Write the question here:

_____

_____

_____

Switch the pen now and allow information to flow...
one word at a time. Remember that no Spirit is going
to come to move your hand! The Wisdom is coming
from Seshat... through the right side of your brain.

Write the response here. Give yourself plenty of
room... as you will write big and sloppy.

Write Seshat's response here:

_____

_____

_____

_____

_____

_____

_____

After you have done that part of the exercise... move
to another question. Put your pen back into the dominant hand, and write this... **Dear Seshat, is there
anything that I can do for you?**

Write the question here:

_____

_____

_____

_____

_____

_____

_____

Switch the pen back to your non-dominant hand and allow the Wisdom to flow... one little word at a time.

Write Seshat's response here:

_____

_____

_____

_____

_____

_____

_____

I suggest that you repeat these two questions daily, until you begin to feel that the information is flowing more easily.

Expect that you are going to write big and sloppy, with the non-dominant hand. **That is perfectly right and good.**

It's important NOT to criticize yourself. And it's important NOT to be concerned that nobody could read this. Nobody else is supposed to read this... except for you. This is your exercise, for your spiritual growth.

This is JUST THE BEGINNING of a relationship with Seshat. It is up to you to continue and formulate more questions until the information flows more smoothly. As you progress, you may find you do not need to ask questions at all. Just sit with pen in hand and invite Seshat to come to you.

You may desire to have more Light on what you have received. Simply repeat the handwriting process asking:

- Will you please give me more clarity on what you said?
- What can I do to communicate with you more effectively?
- Do you see any spiritual or mental blocks? Please let me know what I can do to release/ heal them.

I would love to hear some of your experiences with this... so please drop me a line to tell me how you're doing:

Rebecca@Rebeccamarina.com

Chapter Fifty-one

Afterword from Rebecca

Thank you so much for reading this book. It is my hope that you will use it often and find both Wisdom and Comfort here.

If you enjoyed the material in this book, it shows what an open mind you have!

We are all Light Workers in service to humanity together. I salute you! Namaste!

It would be a pleasure to have you join our online family. You will receive news and updates of all new Thoth materials first.

Visit us at www.rebeccamarina.com/resouces to find many Priceless FREE Meditations.

Printed in Great Britain
by Amazon

34771118R00092